Progressive
POPULAR CLASSICS OF THE GREAT COMPOSERS
VOLUME 5

Arranged by
Jason Waldron

Acknowledgements
Cover: Phil Martin

Distributed by

AUSTRALIA
Koala Publications Pty. Ltd.
37 Orsmond Street,
Hindmarsh 5007
South Australia
Ph: (08) 346 5366
Fax: 61-8-340 9040

USA
Koala Publications Inc.
3001 Redhill Ave.
Bldg 2#109
Costa Mesa
CA. 92626
Ph: (714) 546 2743
Fax: 1-714-546 2749

U.K. and Europe
Music Exchange,
Mail Order Dept,
Claverton Rd, Wythenshawe,
Manchester M23 9NE
Ph: (061) 946 1234
Fax: (061) 946 1195

Order Code KP-P5

ISBN 0 947183 89 2

LIST OF CONTENTS - VOLUME FIVE

Popular Classics of the Great Composers

Arranged by Jason Waldron

FOREWORD

There has always existed a need for a series of books to provide the classical guitarist with a repertoire, long been available to the pianist, of the music most loved by both player and listener alike. The "Progressive Popular Classics" series fills this gap by presenting the music in a clear, concise form.

Teachers will benefit greatly by virtue of being able to substitute teaching pieces written by Carulli, Sor, Giuliani, Carcassi etc. by the well known music of Chopin, Strauss, Tchaikovsky etc. This will allow the student to develop quicker and happier, because each piece would be well known and therefore easier to grasp.

Another important benefit of this series is that the student will acquire an excellent general knowledge of music outside the normal guitar repertoire which will stand him/her in good stead for later study.

TECHNICAL NOTE

1. Fingering is included for all pieces only once and not again for repeated passages.

2. Dynamics and tempo markings have been omitted to allow the player to use his/her own ideas based on the general "feel" of the music.

No. 1

Long, Long Ago

Thomas Bayly (1797-1839)

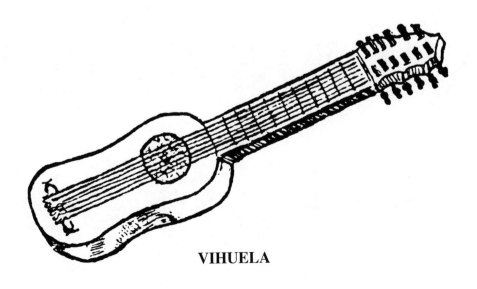

VIHUELA

No. 2   Violin Concerto Theme

Ludwig van Beethoven (1770-1827)

Allegro

No. 3

To a Wild Rose

Edward MacDowell (1861-1908)

Moderato

MACDOWELL

No. 4   Carnival of Venice

Niccolo Paganini (1782-1840)

No. 5
Theme from March Slav

Peter Ilyich Tchaikovsky (1840-1893)

Andante

No. 6

Turkish March

Ludwig van Beethoven (1770-1827)

No. 7 — The Great Gate of Kiev
(from 'Pictures at an Exhibition')

Modest Mussorgsky (1839-1881)

Maestoso

No. 8 Aria from 'The Marriage of Figaro'

Wolfgang Amadeus Mozart (1756-1791)

No. 9   Overture to 'Poet and Peasant'

Franz von Suppe (1819-1895)

Andante maestoso

No. 10   Variations on a Theme by Haydn

Johannes Brahms (1833-1897)

No. 11   # Beautiful Dreamer

Stephen Foster (1826-1864)

Moderato

No. 12
Mighty Lak' A Rose

Ethelbert Nevin (1862-1901)

Andantino

No. 13

Pilgrims Chorus
(from 'Tannhauser')

Richard Wagner (1813-1883)

Andante maestoso

No. 14 Entry of the Gladiators

Julius Fucik (1872-1916)

Allegretto

No. 15   Fingal's Cave

Felix Mendelssohn (1809-1847)

Allegro moderato

No. 16

New World Symphony
(Theme No. 1)

Antonin Dvorak (1841-1904)

Allegro risoluto

No. 17

New World Symphony
(Theme No. 2)

Antonin Dvorak (1841-1904)

Allegretto

No. 18　Hungarian Dance No. 6

Johannes Brahms (1833-1897)

Allegro

No. 19 — Vesti la Giubba

Ruggiero Leoncavallo (1858-1919)

Adagio

No. 20   Slavonic Dance No. 2

Antonin Dvorak (1841-1904)

Allegretto grazioso

No. 21

Serenade for Strings

Peter Ilyich Tchaikovsky (1840-1893)

Moderato

No. 22 When the Stars Were Brightly Shining
(from 'Tosca')

Giacomo Puccini (1858-1924)

Andante

No. 23   Wedding Day

Edvard Grieg (1843-1907)

No. 24

Laughing Song
(from 'Fledermaus')

Johann Strauss (1825-1899)

Allegretto

No. 25   Polonaise

Frederic Chopin (1810-1849)

Allegretto

CHOPIN

No. 26

Theme from William Tell

⑥ = D

Giaocchino Rossini (1792-1868)

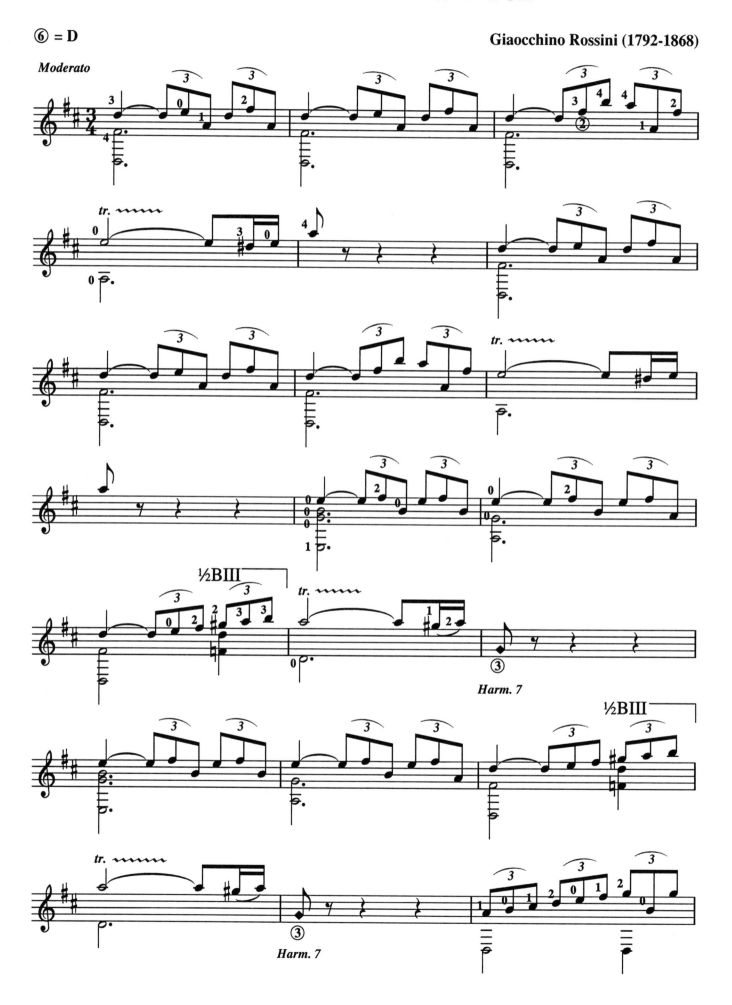

Harm. 7

Harm. 7

No. 27   Mattinata

Ruggiero Leoncavallo (1858-1919)

Moderato

No. 28

Barcarolle
(from 'Tales of Hoffman')

Jacques Offenbach (1819-1880)

⑥ = D

Moderato

No. 29

Wedding March
(from 'Midsummer Night's Dream')

Felix Mendelssohn (1809-1843)

Allegro

No. 30 Overture to 'The Barber of Seville'

Gioacchino Rossini (1792-1868)

Allegro moderato

No. 31   Blue Danube Waltz No. 1

⑥ = D

Johann Strauss (1825-1899)

No. 32

Blue Danube Waltz No. 2

⑥ = D

Johann Strauss (1825-1899)

No. 33

Blue Danube Waltz No. 3

⑥ = D

Johann Strauss (1825-1899)

Moderato

No. 34

Blue Danube Waltz No. 4

Johann Strauss (1825-1899)

⑥ = D

Moderato

No. 35   Blue Danube Waltz No. 5

⑥ = D

Johann Strauss (1825-1899)

Moderato

ROSSINI,
an enthusiastic amateur guitarist.